AVANCER

AVANCER

First edition, 2022
ISBN 978-607-9489-90-8

Ámsterdam 163 A
Colonia Hipódromo, 06100
Ciudad de México
arquine.com

Director
Miquel Adrià

Editor
Brenda Soto Suárez

Design
David Kimura + Gabriela Varela

Translation
Fionn Petch

Proofreading
Quentin Pope

Prepress
Emilio Breton

AVANCER

Macías Peredo + Manuel Cervantes Estudio

Arquine

Table of Contents

9 A Vertical Path: The Context
Oscar Ramírez

29 Conversation with Javier García, Magui Peredo,
Salvador Macías and Manuel Cervantes in San Luis Potosí

50 Plans

70 Construction Process
Excavation
Structure
Enclosures

81 Photographs

116 Bios

119 Credits

Fig. 1.
Armadillo de Los Infante, a town located in the northeast of San Luis Potosí

Text by Oscar Ramírez
Photography by César Béjar

In San Luis Potosí, building vertically was always a luxury rather than a necessity. As a raw material, its wide-open horizons have traced out and flattened down its architectures, merging them with the site.

In the second half of the 16th century, following the Spanish conquest and the Mixtón War in what is now the state of Jalisco, a number of colonization expeditions were carried out. The north of the capital was considered territory known to be occupied by diverse warlike nomadic tribes that hindered access to these regions. The conquistadors also treated all the local indigenous people as 'Chichimecas' without geographical distinction, naming the region 'Gran Chichimeca.' In reality, there were several indigenous groups that moved around continuously, and didn't build houses or cultivate the land. Nor did they build temples or display idolatry, save for a few tribes that worshipped the sun. They ate wild berries and roots, and above all prickly pear and mesquite pods, to which they added a stimulant: peyote (genus *Lophophora*). Where the city of San Luis Potosí now stands, there was once an important center for the Guachichil tribe, known as the 'Gran Tunal' because of the forest of prickly pear bushes that grew close to the mines, providing the fruits in abundance. For the Spanish Empire, this territory was located between the political demarcation of the kingdoms of New Galicia (the present-day states of Jalisco, Nayarit, Aguascalientes and Zacatecas), New León, New Santander, and New Spain itself.

The confrontations between Spaniards and indigenous people grew more belligerent the more that the former ventured into these places. This led to a guerrilla war in the region that lasted for fifty years, between 1550 and 1600. Towards the end of the war, the Spanish opted for a political means of resolving the conflict, by transferring to the north four hundred families of Tlaxcaltecas, who had been their earliest allies, and distributing them across different areas with the intention that their settlement would also pacify the hostile nomad tribes. One of these congregations established itself in a place called Mezquitic, some twenty kilometers from the present-day state capital. From here the first pacification and exploration ventures were begun, leading to the discovery of valuable minerals that could potentially be exploited in a mountain forty kilometers from that site. It was baptized with the name San Pedro del Potosí, a deliberate allusion to the wealth of the mines of Potosí in Upper Peru, now Bolivia. In 1592 the excitement around the mineral discovery led to a significant movement of people who settled a flat area of land with good sources of water close to the mountain, which became known as Puesto de San Luis. By the end of that year, the street plan for the town of Guachichil-Tlaxcalteca was already being laid.

With the grid plan of the town of San Luis Potosí already established, a number of indigenous satellites formed around it. First in 1592 was the village of Nuestra Señora de la Asunción Tlaxcalilla and the Barrio de Santiago, both to the north along the banks of the Santiago river, and to the west the Barrio de Tequisquiapan. A few years later, in 1597, the Pueblo de San Miguel was built on the southern fringes. In the east, the Barrio de Montecillo was built in 1600, and finally the Barrio de San Sebastián in the south-east in 1603, consolidating the outer districts as a predominantly indigenous belt. Towards the end of the 17th century the Puesto de San Juan de Guadalupe was founded alongside the Españita river on the southern flank of Pueblo de San Miguel, by then known as the Barrio de San Miguelito.

The settlement of the pueblos and peripheral neighborhoods of San Luis was determined, in the first place, by the natural frontiers of the Santiago river to the north and its bifurcation towards the south and east, where it is known as the Españita river, and subsequently by the Caminos Reales (Royal Roads) heading to the four points of the compass: to Mexico City in the south, to Cerro de San Pedro in the east, to Zacatecas in the north, and to Guadalajara in the west. At no specific moment in time, and as a result of the natural growth of each district or pueblo, the various settlements merged to form a single city that retains its original street layout. The historical downtown area can be read as a checkerboard pattern, with a now barely recognizable organization by sectors and the present-day suburban neighborhoods that gather like segments around it, with marked irregularities where they intersect. The royal title that granted it the name of City was conceded by the King of Spain in 1650, one of the last major cities in Mexico to obtain this ranking.

The mining industry made it necessary to build processing plants for the material extracted from the ground. Unlike in the neighboring mining centers of Guanajuato and Zacatecas, where the process used the amalgamation technique, in the newly founded center of San Luis Potosí the smelting process was used in the early years, which required buildings to be constructed on watercourses or below reservoirs to provide the necessary resources.

Figs. 2–3.
Armadillo de Los Infante

Figs. 4–5.
Ruins in the town of Cerro de San Pedro

Meanwhile, the need for then-scarce charcoal and firewood to fire the smelting furnaces led to the construction of a network of roads to meet the growing fuel requirements. As a result the so-called Haciendas de Beneficio or estates built around a smelter sprang up in a rather haphazard manner, with a high demand for new land for construction sites.

The Haciendas de Beneficio were mainly built in the north and west of San Luis Potosí, as well as in the other villages around Cerro de San Pedro. Since the central part of the city had been established with residential neighborhoods, the semi-organized development of these production complexes became an early 'industrial zone' with its necessary operational thoroughfares. Growth in mining activity led to a search for new territories, further away but better situated and with more natural resources available, for the foundation of haciendas. As a result, primitive housing models were established for the emerging landowners, together with productive and work spaces, which varied significantly. Sometimes all the spaces required were gathered into a single structure, while other times they were kept separate, though connected as a complex or within a single fenced area. In the present-day village of Monte Caldera, located seven kilometers north of the Cerro de San Pedro, remains of such settlements can still be seen.

The urgency to establish haciendas quickly helped to meet the demand for production in the mines of Cerro de San Pedro. At the same time it opened up opportunities for prosperity throughout the region. It was not long before the hacienda model became a self-contained micro-city: a living organism where all the parts acted together and in proportion. Analyzed from a social perspective, the hacienda structure generated mutual dependency among its inhabitants, who were all involved in its subsistence and growth.

At the same time, if the city of San Luis Potosí was configured on the basis of the division of neighborhoods that coexisted and competed in every sense, in every region the haciendas would maintain a similar competitive spirit, something that is reflected in their architecture and layout. An item of data that clarifies the situation is this: most of the large landowners and their families enjoyed a dual life, with a residence in their haciendas and a building in the city too.

In most haciendas in the region, their similarities and influences are clear, with the qualification that the larger they were, the more defined the public spaces and buildings, such as plazas, church, roads and so on. As a result, for at least 300 years the spaces in a hacienda were the private property of a single person or family, a successful balance where the community didn't quite become a village or, as in many cases, need fortress-like walls to confine it.

The layouts of the haciendas vary greatly, the form depending on the type of production. All have at least a series of constant and classifiable spaces: a large house for the landowner's residence with administrative spaces; chapel or church to provide religious services to the whole community; a company store selling goods not produced by the hacienda itself; silos; stables; a public square for gatherings; and walls, built in some areas for security.

In Mexico there is no clear data on the number of haciendas that existed or that persist today. The hacienda system was legally destroyed by the agrarian reform that, between 1934 and 1940, redistributed some twenty-five million hectares of hacienda-owned land to *ejidos* (collective land tenure arrangements). As a result, most of them were dismantled or otherwise transformed. The largest haciendas prospered as villages or were absorbed into cities. Most such complexes, no longer in operation or impossible to maintain, now lie in ruins or have disappeared altogether.

In the case of San Luis Potosí, the number is not clear either but they can be divided into three geographical regions. These are the Huasteca zone on the Gulf plain, almost at sea level; the intermediate zone around one thousand meters above sea level; and the Altiplano zone, which is divided in turn into the Altiplano and San Luis itself. Given the strong connection with the centrality of the state capital, a number of aspects where the tendency to build taller structures is of interest.

The churches or chapels in the haciendas are the most frequent, with bell towers that for practical reasons are built tall so that the pealing of bells can be heard from a distance. This important requirement led to multiple solutions that competed in height and ornament. There are three bell tower types: churches with either one or two towers flanking the main façade, and churches with a single bell tower that also forms the façade, that is, where the tower structure itself becomes the narthex or vestibule of the nave. The latter type, which is more original, is found in a number of churches set fairly far apart. Of note are the chapel at the Hacienda Santa Teresa, as well as that of Peotillos, of San Diego del Rioverde and of the Santuario de San José, within the city itself. Notable examples of chapels with one or two towers include Pozo del Carmen, built by the Carmelites, as was that of La Parada, and in Valle de San Francisco the chapels on the Gogorrón and Bledos haciendas. One of the most influential and significant is at the state boundary in Jaral de Berrio.

When it comes to the main house, there are three examples of particular interest: La Sauceda, Peotillos and Pozo del Carmen. La Sauceda was one of the first haciendas to be founded, in the late 16th century. It occupies a gentle ridge alongside a ravine, below the Sierra de Álvarez to the east of San Luis valley, some thirty-five kilometers from the capital. Its mining origins began with the infrastructure to process the minerals extracted from the San Pedro mountain. With the passage of the centuries, the focus of production switched to mezcal, and in the 19th century it developed one of the largest such facilities. The core of the hacienda complex, with a public plaza, main house and church was the first to be built and was gradually altered over the years. The final expansion and completion of the complex was in the 19th century. The principal building or main house stands independently from the church and has a projecting portico formed of eight arches topped with an ornamental brick parapet, comprising the vestibule that in turn provides a base for an emblematic and distinctive lookout tower that establishes the symmetry of the building and accentuates the hierarchy of the main entrance. The generous courtyard is surrounded by a covered walkway lined by a series of slender arches and columns. Today it is abandoned and at severe risk of collapse.

Peotillos is a hacienda whose name alludes to the abundance of the peyote cactus. It is located in Villa de Hidalgo some sixty kilometers north of the state capital, on the flanks of the Sierra de Guadalcázar. After its foundation in the mid-17th century, it was dedicated to the production and sale of small livestock and to ixtle, a vegetable fiber extracted from the agave cactus. In the following centuries, the complex had different owners. One was Nicolás Fernando Torres, a wealthy merchant and mine owner who left no descendants, but bequeathed the hacienda to the Carmelite religious order, who expanded the complex with large barns and connected it with the adjacent hacienda Pozo del Carmen, which also belonged to the order. By the 19th century it had changed owner and use, now expanded and refurbished for mezcal production. It was in this period that the most significant alterations were made, giving it a more ornamental appearance. The single-story main house is located along one side of the public plaza and forms a complex with the same height and ornament as the inverted arches of the façade parapet. As in La Sauceda, there is a notable tower of similar proportions used as a lookout, together with a five-arch porch that forms a vestibule for the courtyard of the house. Inside, the open space gathers all the rooms on a single floor, distributing them around the perimeter by means of a broad porticoed walkway, adorned with blue-hued paintings on all the walls.

The Hacienda de Pozo del Carmen, located twenty-five kilometers to the south of Peotillos, is another of the properties bequeathed to the Carmelite order. In this case, two later, separate constructions form a significant extension. The initial phase, known as the old house, comprises as well as the landowner's residence an atrium, chapel with sacristy, and a waterwheel. This chapel contains a golden Baroque altarpiece, and has a Latin cross layout with two axes, a transept and apse, together with a bell tower formed of two volumes and topped with a lantern. The building known as the new house, meanwhile, is very similar in style to that at Peotillos and at La Sauceda. It is a single-story building in the form of a quadrangle with a fortress-like appearance. The main façade is formed from a containing wall that delineates the entire building with vertical openings reaching the ground, narrow windows in line with the walls and with no other ornamentation than the cantilevered sills. The wall is topped by a sinuous inverted arcade forming a crest. A broad porch flanked by an arcade with carved stone columns contains the main entrance, ensuring the sobriety of the building. Inside the symmetrical floor plan is divided in two, with a small main courtyard. Some segments of the building have two floors, including a prominent lookout tower with an octagonal base and ogive windows situated over the principal rooms in the southern wing.

The chimney stacks of some haciendas became a significant vertical element and formed landmarks. Notable examples built with brick include those of haciendas of Gogorrón, Jesús María, Peñasco and Real de Catorce, stone-built examples are found at the haciendas of Bledos, Bocas, Vallumbroso and La Trinidad. The latter has an enigmatic, sculptural spiral staircase that ascends the three distinct sections of the chimney.

In the state capital, the work of Carlos Suárez Fiallo came to prominence in the late 19th century. His best known work is the former penitentiary, today converted into the Centenario Arts Center. Yet Suárez was also responsible for a number of urban and architectural projects, some only as builder or indeed inventor. Originally from Veracruz, there is no record of his educational background, though he clearly displayed a knowledge and practice of civil engineering and architecture. Carlos Morán de la Rosa describes him as a figure who 'more than ingenious and creative, though he was both of those things, proved to be determined and persevering. He patented various artifacts of his own invention, such as the apparatus to extract minerals by amalgamation that he delivered to the mining company of Concepción, in Real de Catorce; or the Santa Teresa coffins, famous in their day. He also introduced steam power to carpenter's workshops, and later expanded its application to nixtamal and cacao mills; and even invented a games mechanism known as *Frontón de Salón* ("Lounge Wallball").'[1]

1. Carlos Morán De la Rosa, 'Carlos Suárez Fiallo. Precursor de la arquitectura porfiriana', *Revista La Corriente*, San Luis Potosí, 2013.

Fig. 6.
Chimney stack, La Trinidad mezcal factory

Figs. 7–8.
Former penitentiary—now the San Luis Potosí Centenario Arts Center—built by Carlos Suárez Fiallo, remodeled by Taller 6A

Suárez Fiallo was involved as a partner in numerous enterprises and was a councilor on the San Luis Potosí city council. It may be that his political positions helped him with the organization and promotion of projects benefitting the city, such as the urban infrastructure works on Carranza avenue, a poorhouse and the penitentiary.

In 1878 he purchased the existing public baths originally known as 'Ánimas' then upon the change of owner as 'Quiñones' before finally acquiring the name of the San José Baths. The engineer also bought the adjacent lots, which he amalgamated to form a single property with an irregular perimeter connecting the parallel streets of Ignacio López Rayón and Pascual M. Hernández, in the city center. As owner of this land, he designed a new building for the baths, constructing a tower to provide gravity-fed water. The three-section brick tower stands out in the city, with the only clear view from Pascual M. Hernández street, where the façade is completely blind without any access to the baths, leaving only a series of tall and narrow windows and a public sundial still visible today. With a strong eclectic influence of the period, the octagonal tower is ornamented with neo-Arab motifs and pointed polylobulate arches. A railing at the top suggests that it may have been used as a lookout point. From the main entrance on López Rayón street, the building presents a series of courtyards and offers a plinth for the tower, seen to the rear. A few years later, in 1883, Suárez Fiallo designed the City Penitentiary and began its construction prior to the infamous Lecumberri prison in Mexico City, and the projects by architect Lorenzo de la Hidalga, one of the most significant of the time. In this project, the engineer fully expressed the utilitarian philosophy of the panopticon, invented by British thinker Jeremy Bentham in the late 18th century, which comprises a space allowing a warden to observe all the prisoners from a central tower, with the result that they are constantly aware of being watched. The building is divided into three areas. To the rear is an open space used as an exercise yard. The central section is the area of observation and vigilance, with a prominent tower in the center and eight concentric sections like the spokes of a wheel, with a perimeter walkway that confines the space with a double stone ashlar wall. The space to the front is occupied by the first courtyard and main entrance, flanked by two robust towers. The complex is contained within continuous stone ashlar walls measuring over ten meters in height. The severe aspect of the exterior is interrupted by the watchtowers, with battlements located at each corner of the building that are almost independent protrusions. The building was inaugurated in 1904, although it had already been operating for some years, and it remained under construction for several years without all of the intended spaces inside being completed. The upper floors of four of the eight sections were never built.

The period we know as the Porfiriato triggered the development of numerous public buildings that would transform the city of San Luis. The railroad lines that connected with the north of the country—in particular with Laredo—generated significant progress throughout the region, making the city one of the most important destinations in Mexico. At the turn of the century a modest station had been constructed on the north side of the central Alameda park and it operated successfully for several decades. Later in the Porfiriato period, with a taste for eclecticism in full swing, it was demolished and replaced with a second station, opened in 1914 but damaged by fire in 1920. Despite its ruinous state it continued to operate until the late 1930s when Manuel Ortiz Monasterio (Mexico City, 1887–1967) designed a new station on the same site as its predecessors. With experience working on the Durango railroad station in 1925, a more discrete edifice in a classical style, the architect Monasterio designed a more ambitious project with Art Deco influences never seen before in the city, and probably one of the best in the country. The steel structure enabled a slender building with significant open spaces that brought modernity to the terminal. The station comprises two main volumes. The first functions as a broad triple-height gallery that contains the public spaces: waiting rooms, ticket office, and store. The second is a three-story building for the station offices, with a prominent tower attached to it that rises to seven stories. This structure, specifically designed to contain a double-height bay, houses a singular clock mechanism that can simultaneously move all the hands on the four clock faces on the tower's façades, meaning they can be seen from every direction. The building was inaugurated in late 1942 as a celebration of the modernity brought by the railroad.

Between 1965 and 1968 Enrique de la Mora y Palomar (b. Guadalajara, 1907; d. Mexico City, 1978) invited Félix Candela (b. Madrid, 1910; d. Raleigh, 1997) to work on the project for three churches designed and built almost simultaneously. The first was the Church of Santa Cruz in the Industrial Aviación neighborhood, where they designed a building with a diamond-shaped floor plan and a roof spanning 54 meters that was inspired by a nun's headpiece or hat. The church's geometry is regular, with two straight-edged hyperbolic paraboloids four centimeters thick and joined by beams that allow the entry of light from overhead. This was no new experiment for the pair, as they had built a similar church five years earlier in Monterrey, although on a different scale.

Meanwhile, the Colegio México Chapel is a building that has a triangular floor plan with a curved edged that breaks down the geometric form in its walls and roof. Three supports converted into inverted beams support the fifteen-meter height of the building while holding up the roof, formed of three hyperbolic paraboloids that intersect the walls with horizontal stained glass windows.

Finally, a third project developed by this pair in Barrio de Tequisquiapan, known today as the Parroquia de Nuestra Señora de los Remedios, has a roof formed of four hyperbolic paraboloids joined by a metal structure at the apex. Even as a building of larger dimensions than the two previous ones, its siting with two adjacent buildings detracts from the expressive geometry of the roof, as these force a partial perspective that emphasizes a descending view in terms of the building's proportions. From the inside, the experience and sensation is radically different.

For decades, the power exerted by the historic center and original residential neighborhoods generated a certain timidity, and new architecture only brought contemporaneity to San Luis Potosí with quiet decorum. The industrial potential developed freely in the peripheries with utilitarian success, but largely containing a natural expansion of the urban area. Towards the end of the 20th century, the city's expansion towards the west became a kind of canvas where the most striking urban and architectural exercises to date have been concentrated. One of the first of these, the Tangamanga Park, was developed in 1985 and soon became one of the most important urban amenities on the south and west of the city. At approximately 420 hectares, it remains one of the largest public parks in the country while being a powerful and attractive amenity for the growth of the city towards the flanks of the El Potosí mountain. At one end of the park, once the furthest limit of the city, the Interactive Museum Labyrinth of Sciences and Arts was built, opened in 2008 and designed by Ricardo Legorreta (Mexico City, 1931–2012). The project reinterprets a typical main house of a hacienda to insert itself in the landscape of the city, using contemporary forms and clad in a local stone known as *sangre de pichón* or 'pigeon blood,' the red hues helping to integrate with its surroundings. The galleries form a set of volumes around a central courtyard and include a thirty-five-meter tower housing a telescope and lookout point.

A sound space was added a year after the museum opened, with a different style of architecture altogether. The Acoustic Pavilion of the Museum Labyrinth of Sciences and Arts is a project by Taller de Arquitectura | Mauricio Rocha with sound interventions by Manuel Rocha Iturbide, and is built in the ruins of a firing range, part of a former military barracks just meters from the museum. Taking advantage of the shape and length of an existing stone wall, three 'C'-shaped wall enclose an interior space ten meters wide that incorporates an existing tree. A flat roof support itself on the long walls and projects over an exposed concrete pavement, where two benches position the stage for the acoustic work that reproduces the sound of birds from the highlands of San Luis Potosí state. The pavilion is camouflaged with its surroundings and the landscape

Fig. 9.
Interactive Museum Labyrinth of Sciences and Arts, Ricardo Legorreta

with walls built in local stone that merge with those of the ruins thanks to their material similarity, and the absence of paths or signage marking a route. Perhaps without even intending to, the museum has charted the way forward for the city's development in the forthcoming years.

At the end of the century, in March 1999, the aforementioned City Penitentiary relocated its inmates and close its doors. The building in the heart of the city was left abandoned until in 2004 an initial academic and artistic design was put forward for a new Arts Center for the city to occupy it. With a clear idea and detailed program of requirements, the same year a national architecture competition was called, and won by Alejandro Sánchez García's Taller 6A studio. His proposal consisted of a subtle, conservation-oriented intervention by means of giving new life to the cells as essential spaces in the building, transforming them into larger spaces better suited to the new architectural program that aimed to erase the stigma attached to the complex. The original project for the prison was completed with the construction of the unbuilt upper floors of four of the eight sections, replicating the barrel vaults of the original volumes in exposed concrete. The alterations made to the walls over the years were removed, revealing the original ashlars, and remaking the interior spaces. Each of the blocks of stone was removed and relocated outside, creating new walls and exterior spaces. The eight triangular patios formed by the spokes of the panopticon were each given a unique design, establishing a link with the activities indoors. Planters, fountains, paths and low walls form a single open complex that connects with the perimeter path. The final result is a building that transforms the former use of the prison without altering its layout or original appearance.

Meanwhile, to the northwest is located an industrial zone where for over one hundred years a copper plant operated, ending production in 2010. The vast 450-hectare area belonging to Industrial Minera México, S.A. de C.V. (IMMSA) contained, as well as the factory, industrial areas and infrastructure that operated for many years on what was the edge of the city. Upon its closure, Mario Schjetnan's Grupo de Diseño Urbano developed the IMMSA Plan for the transformation of the site and a new multi-purpose development. The project comprised three parts: a linear public park and plant nursery, two structures for the containment of contaminated soils, and landscaping of the clinker deposits. The San Luis Potosí Bicentenary Park is the first stage of the IMMSA master plan to be built and avails of the coincidence in time between the conversion of the complex and the mood of celebration around the bicentenary of Mexican independence to adopt a name and grant new meaning to the zone. The almost nine-hectare linear park bounds the complex and comprises recreational spaces, cycle paths and water bodies that complement the layout of the development. A subtle and effective reworking of the topography at different heights establishes a visual relationship with the former industrial zone along the route. Meanwhile, the rest of the plan involved a six-year process of soil remediation and cleansing, together with structures being recycled and reinserted in the city, forming a new territory rather than a boundary. The treatment of the landscape is sober and subtle but not minimal, with notable features including the scattered presence of chimneys from the industrial ruins, and two pyramids created to contain the contaminated soils. Both four-sided, truncated pyramidal structures formed by embankments of local stone merge with the landscape and provide a uniform color across the complex, while the stairs and ramps intersect to form contrasts with the ocher-hued paving, delineating their irregular geometry in plan view. This combination of natural materials and colors is replicated in slopes across the entire project and on different scales, constructing a landscape that is transformed but also returned to nature.

Avancer Tower, by Magui Peredo, Salvador Macías and Manuel Cervantes, is located in between these two great blocks that flank the western side of the city and matches the landscape out of which it emerges, between residential developments that trace the topography of the zone and an expanding urban infrastructure. It joins an uncertain and fast-moving architectural horizon dressed with the colors of the earth and with the echo of all that surrounds it, with a façade that points in all directions, but especially to the vertical.

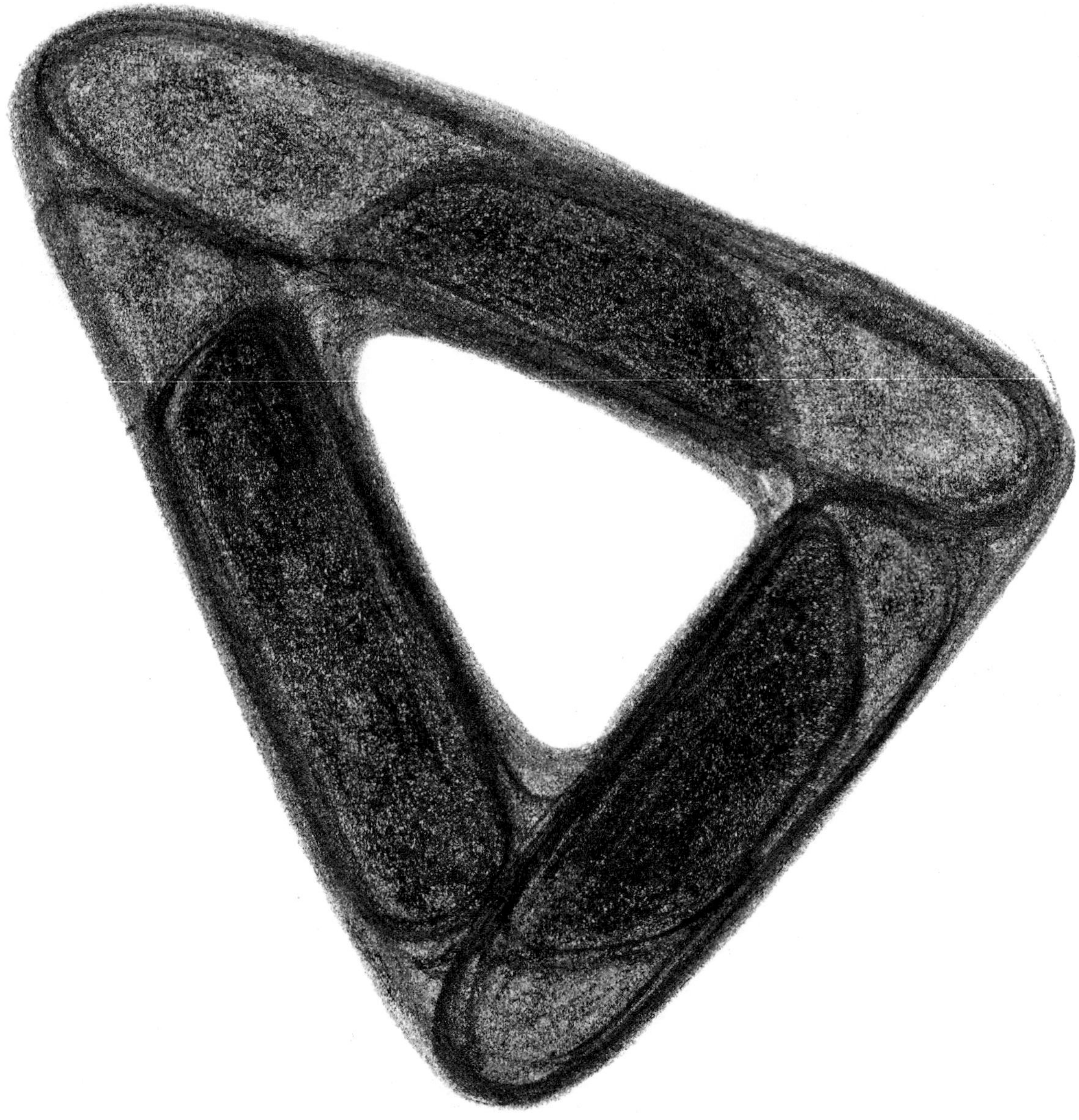

Conversation with Javier García, Magui Peredo, Salvador Macías and Manuel Cervantes in San Luis Potosí

MIQUEL ADRIÀ

What prompted the decision to build a corporate headquarters for your company?

JAVIER GARCÍA

The aim was to improve the city, starting with the fact that San Luis Potosí has long been a strategic point in Mexico, an industrial hub. The automobile assembly plants and other industries that arrived here don't generate an economic spillover in the city. They provide a lot of jobs, but they don't create that ripple effect because they are French, German or US companies and so the profits return to their headquarters. The jobs tend to be low-income rather than middle-income level. So I asked myself, what can we do to encourage better-paid employment? Usually, university graduates move to the big cities: to the capital, to Monterrey, to Guadalajara, and more recently to Querétaro, which has come to the fore since all the corporations leaving Mexico City have set up there. So we asked ourselves why that is. In San Luis Potosí there is no space for such companies, ones that are not doing manufacturing but need room for their back offices. We carried out market research and we saw that there is a credible interest on the part of these types of companies in investing here. Some had their back offices in India. We decided that, if we were going to offer such a space, then it has to be a quality, disruptive space that was functional and that would become a landmark. It also has to age with grace and to deserve its location at the highest point in the city at the intersection of two major avenues. On top of that, it has to reflect a younger generation of people who are putting forward new and fresh ideas. The previous generation did this with another type of architecture, with the haciendas of the Hoteles Quinta Real for example, while we wanted an architecture that reflects the local identity, a more contemporary architecture that doesn't fall out of fashion but endures.

MA

I'm surprised by the fact that together with your interest in a contemporary design, you are also so clear about wanting it to be timeless. These are two concepts that can sometimes be contradictory, but transcending time is very important to you.

JG

I'm an enemy of patch repairs, and I'm a perfectionist. I prefer to do things right first time around. Otherwise, everything becomes more expensive and the dignity of the project is lost.

MANUEL CERVANTES

Both Javier and his family were always very clear that they wanted the building to be a family legacy to San Luis Potosí. This meant that it had to age well.

JG

That's right, it was always conceived as a legacy project.

MA

Why did you decide to hold a competition and invite certain architects who, at first glance, weren't obvious choices? None of them had built a corporate office building before...

JG

I was very clear about my own involvement. Although I studied finance, art and architecture have always interested me and have played a major role in my life thanks to my mother. I wanted it to be a young, emerging studio with a promising future. And if I invited better-known firms, my opportunity to be involved would probably be lower. I made a shortlist and I went to Mexico City where I whittled down the list to just three studios I'd not previously heard of: Macías Peredo from Guadalajara, Jorge Covarrubias and Manuel Cervantes from Mexico City. I went to see them in order to get to know them. People asked me: 'Why aren't you approaching Sordo Madaleno or Legorreta?'

MA

How did you find them? How did you select them?

JG

I asked around, I explored the work they'd done. The level of detail of their work made a lot of sense to me. I understood them to be as contemporary as they are Mexican. We carried out a market study that defined the 10,000 m^2 program of office space with parking and retail spaces. I personally went to visit the candidates, and subsequently they made site visits.

MC

The three shortlisted studios met and we persuaded the clients to change the conditions of the project, extending the deadlines and the fees without increasing the overall cost, at the cost of the executive project. That's where we found out who we all were and who we were working for.

SALVADOR MACÍAS

At that time, we were working on the project for a house in San Luis Potosí. We had already done some research into the place, its culture, local construction systems and materials, and Jorge Covarrubias had built some houses there. We didn't know Manuel Cervantes well, but we understood each other. We had crossed paths at conferences, we had both published books with Arquine and we knew each other's work. When we heard that Manuel was invited to the competition, we understood the profile that Javier was seeking for the project. During our site visit, the three participants ate lunch together and we discussed the changes to the competition conditions, asking for more time and a larger budget, at the cost of the executive project fees for the winner.

MA

At what point did the two of you decide to work together?

SM

It was Manuel who took the initiative. He told us that he knew our work; that he thought the Montessori School we built with Erick Pérez in Mazatlán was an interesting, fresh and novel project; and that it was clear that working together with other studios helps refresh ideas. Around about that time, we met up in Mexico City at the MEXTRÓPOLI Festival. We agreed to submit a proposal together, to work on the two proposals, and that each office would develop an idea proposed by both.

MC

So each of us developed a project. We met up several times in Mexico City and Guadalajara. Each idea was distinct. There is always a clash between the project that you like and the one that is most convenient, but in this case we had the chance to bring both parts together. The winning proposal that was built is the one that met the program requirements, and the other proposal was more daring in this sense. To ensure that we felt we were a part of both projects, the studio that developed one project prepared the model for the other.

MA

So in the end, they came and presented their projects. What did you see in each of them, Javier?

JG

A jury was formed comprising engineers, architects and a financial team, each offering something of value. The three proposals were analyzed, taking into account everything from the efficiency of the layout to the creation of a landmark building on a triangular site. The evaluation process was recorded in a score sheet that assessed the virtues of each project. The winner was the most efficient one that best expressed the spirit of San Luis Potosí, interpreting the history of a mining town in a contemporary mode. I went to Guadalajara to tell the architects Salvador and Magui that they had won with the proposal they had presented. That was when they told me that Manuel was also involved in the project. I thought this was brilliant, as it was a way of setting aside their egos in order to work together.

MA

It added value for you, without imposing a specific team.

JG

Adding value, without having to pay double.

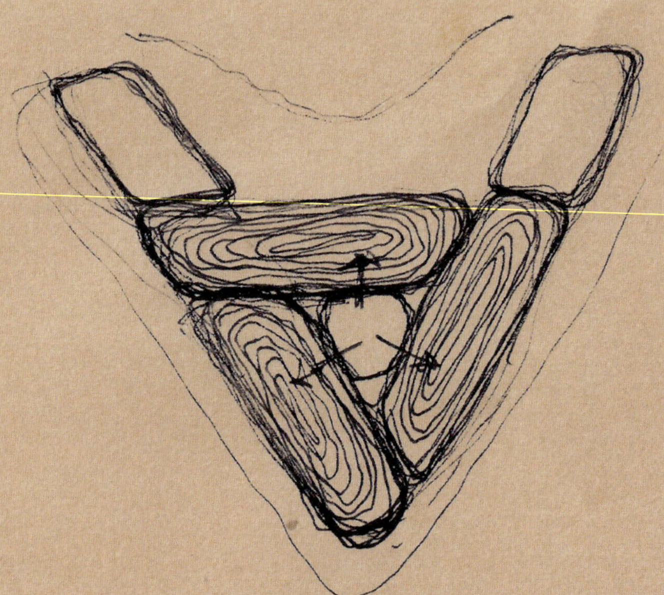

MA

You've mentioned the importance of the building being a part of San Luis Potosí, of belonging to its architectural heritage. Why is that so important? And what is there of San Luis in this project?

MAGUI PEREDO

We love traveling around Mexico, discovering ruins, or in this case, the villages, haciendas and ghost towns that are scattered everywhere in the desert, such as the Cerro de San Pedro, near San Luis Potosí. The colonial downtown area of the city is also extraordinary. Manuel knows this area very well. Meanwhile, we already knew the guidelines for local developments that required buildings to be white, and other criteria that in our view have little to do with San Luis Potosí. We believe that these fail to understand the particular characteristics of the site: the ruins, the rusted scaffolding of the mines and the railings in the center, the warm hues of the pink cantera stone.

MA

In your view, what characterizes the architecture of San Luis Potosí?

SM

Prior to the Spanish colonization, the desert where the city now stands was just a desert, no one lived here. There were no significant human settlements.

MC

A stopping-place...

SM

San Luis was founded by the Spaniards on the Cerro de San Pedro, as a mining town. All the original settlements and haciendas were connected in some way to mining or at least built close to the mines. In fact, the big voids in the city are a reflection of this. What today is the Tangamanga Park or the Minera México are good examples: open sites, lacking in vegetation and with low density where only a few chimneys, ruins, or rusting steel constructions can be seen. Where the bedrock is exposed to view.

MC

On the other hand we have the Historic Center with its cantera stone and colonial architecture. We also looked closely at what other architects had done before us, such as Legorreta or Mauricio Rocha with his sound pavilion, a minimalist intervention with an interesting awareness of the site's materials. There is also the Arts Center by Alejandro Sánchez that, although it is a restoration and intervention, shows a clear understanding of the place. So between what we found in the Historic Center and the contemporary interpretations we knew personally, clues appeared that helped us to see the value of the place, far from the generic conditions applied to new constructions on the outskirts.

SM

San Luis Potosí has a very well-preserved colonial Historic Center, with its original stone paving slabs and a lot of character. It is an impeccable site and one we have learned a lot from. The floors at the entrance to Avancer Tower recall this character of the paving on the Calzada de Guadalupe, for example.

MA

So to turn to the project itself, what are the ideas you want to pick out? I understand that, on the one hand, there is an excavation that links to the local history of mining...

MC

Chronologically, we must remember that we had to deliver the executive project in order to embark on the work, and we asked Javier how long the excavation would take. At that point he estimated it would take at least a year, so we proposed that we make use of that time to develop the executive project.

JG

In the end it was eighteen months of excavation, which meant we didn't have to race...

MC

And also to create a sense of collaboration between client and architects to develop the project properly. The usual situation among developers is the opposite: the developer, contractor, engineer and architect each look out for their respective areas and the only goal is to save money. In this regard, Javier always said 'let's see how we can make it possible to do what you want to do; we'll find the right price, the time, and the ability.' This excavation was the trigger for a strategy to take the time and care we needed to study the proposal properly.

MA

From the outset, did you imagine that the excavation would remain exposed?

SM

We planned to leave a natural embankment, with exposed bedrock. When we realized that the rock could support a vertical face without the need for embankments, we decided to leave it as it was. It's also important to point out that the form of the site defines the shape of the building. I don't think any of us would have proposed a building with curves if the form of the site itself wasn't boomerang-shaped. When Javier called us the first time, he made clear that it wasn't an easy site. There is a twelve-meter gradient from one side of the site to the other. The triangular geometry left a void to the rear, which is what we expected to leave as a natural slope.

MC

The geometry is determined by the site, and the form derives from the building norms that define the height of the tower.

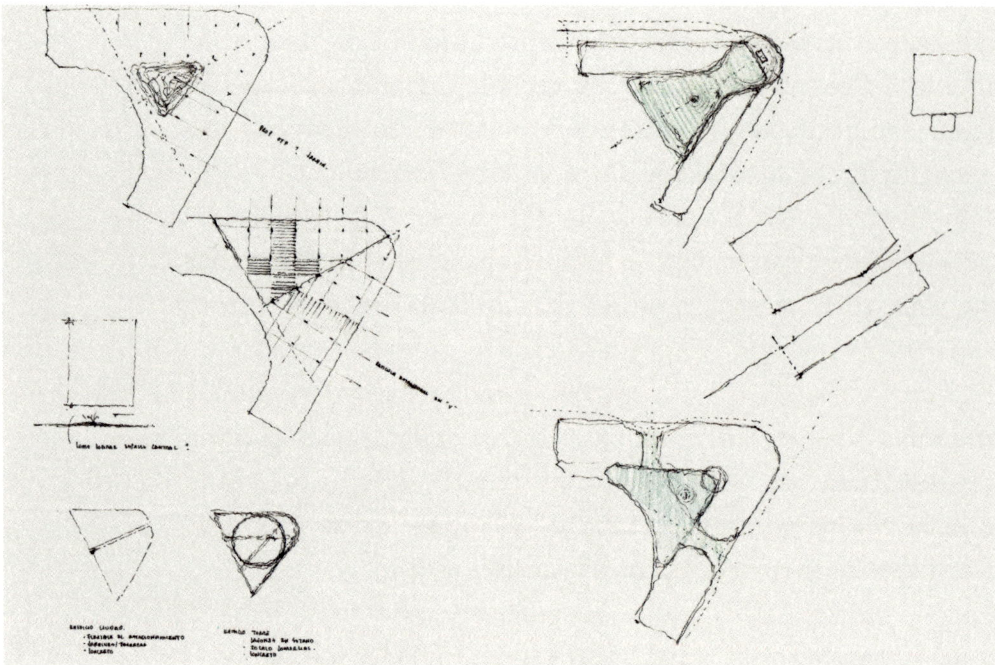

MA

The form is the extrusion of the geometry, and the volumes are terraced in the way that certain Expressionist and Art Deco buildings from the 1930s are, while the tower loses volume as it rises, in the manner of skyscrapers…

SM

It reminds me of something you once said about Mario Pani, who, with a reduced program and only a few square meters of land to play with, built some slender towers that were known at the time as 'mini-skyscrapers'.

MA

Pani also employed this technique of dividing or grooving the façades in such a way that you can't tell just by looking how many floors his buildings have. This is the case here in Avancer Tower too.

JG

The original project was shorter and wider.

MC

That's right, we reduced the surface area and increased the height in order not to exceed the permitted total built area. And the setbacks aim to give it a more slender appearance.

SM

From the outset, Javier asked that the building be an icon in the landscape of the city, which is why the height was important in order to terrace the offices. Each floor receives a terrace or roof garden. In essence, the floor plan is very simple: three bays set around the central, triangular nucleus. Another important request was that it not be like so many office buildings that are all interiors behind

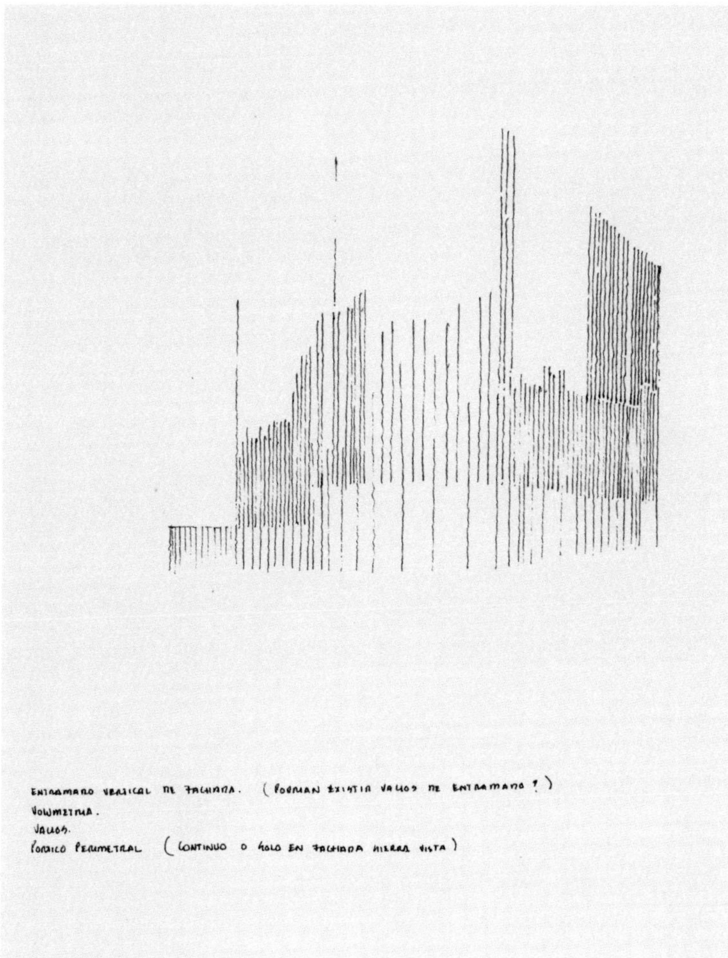
ENTRAMADO VERTICAL DE FACHADA. (PODRIAN EXISTIR VANOS DE ENTRAMADO ?)
VOLUMETRIA.
VANOS.
PORTICO PERIMETRAL (CONTINUO O SOLO EN FACHADA TIERRA VISTA)

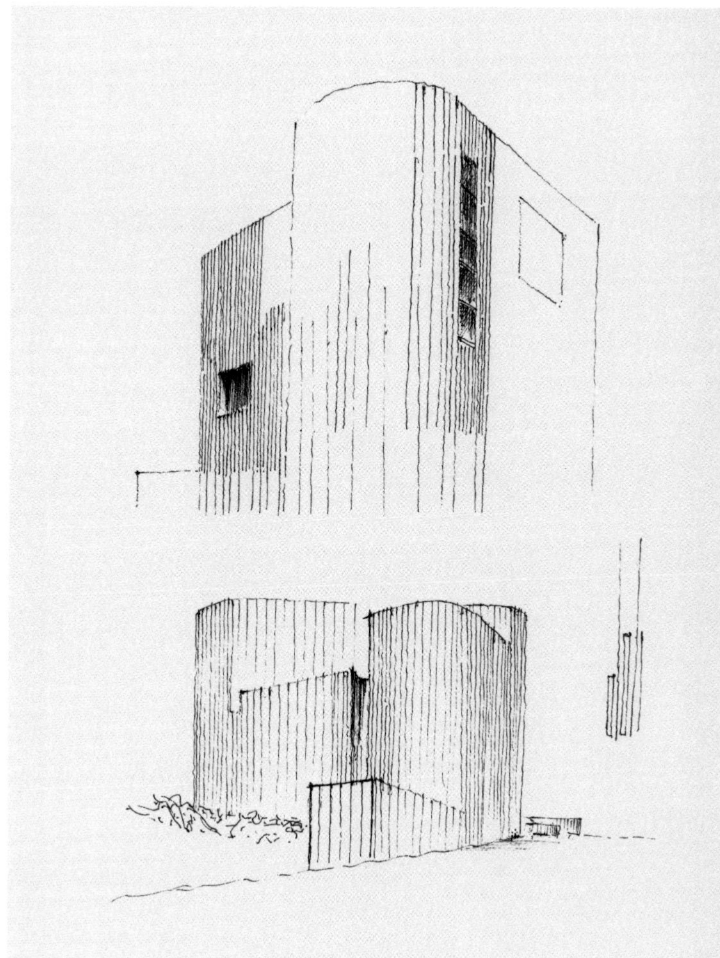

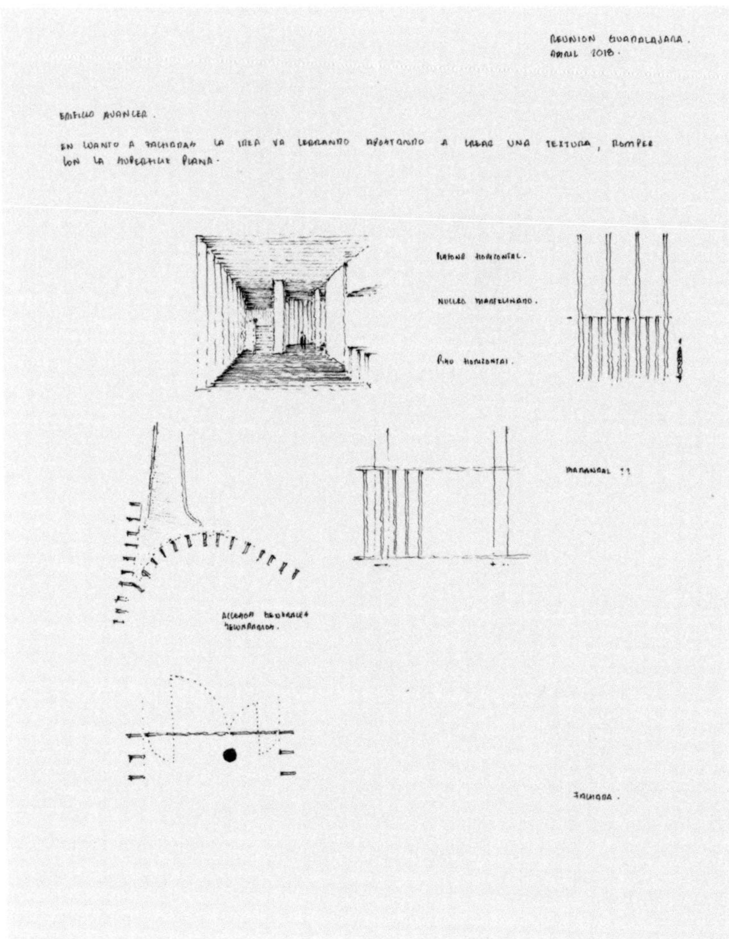
REUNION GUADALAJARA.
ABRIL 2018.
FACHADA.

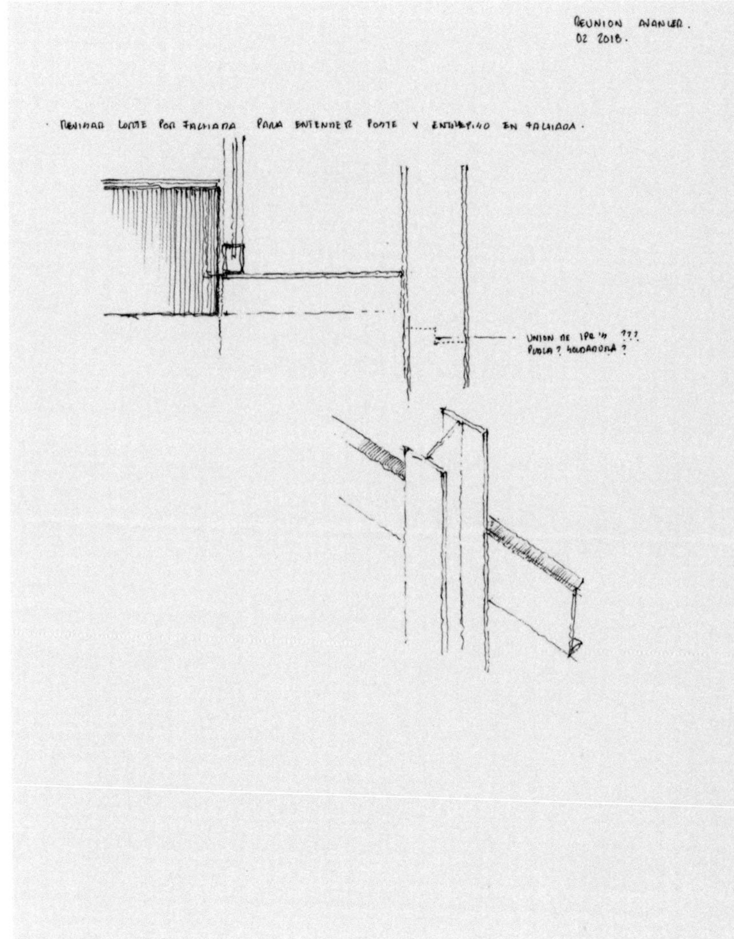
REUNION AVANCER.
02 2018.

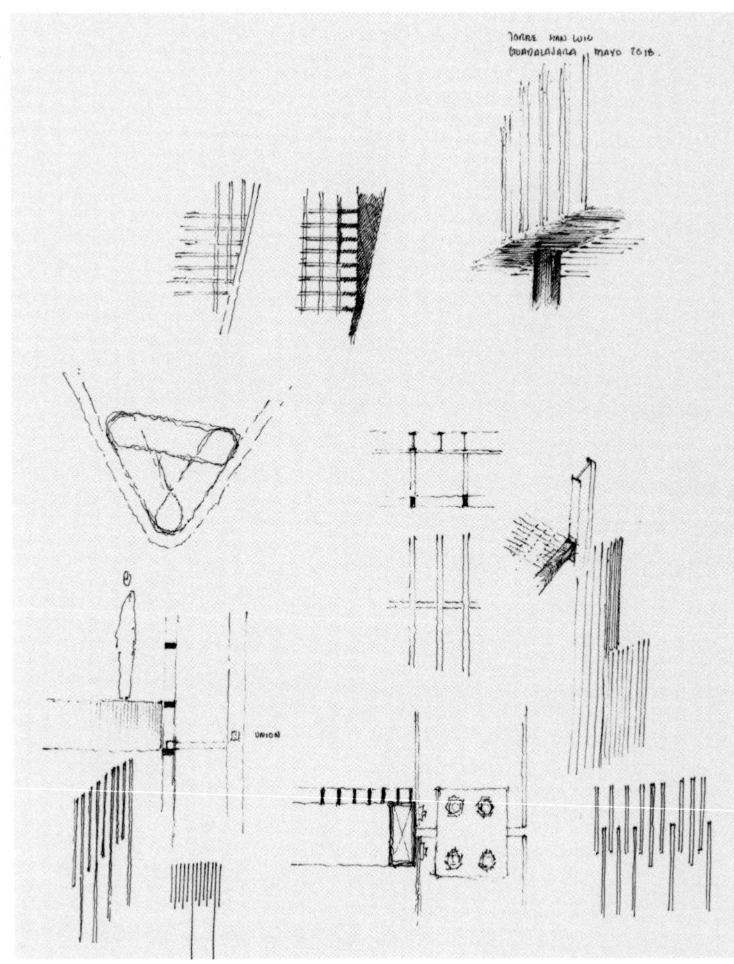
GUADALAJARA MAYO 2018.
UNION

a glass curtain wall. In contrast, here we have these terraces at different heights. This final proposal, unlike the other two in the competition, fosters a relationship between interior and exterior that works really well in a climate like that of San Luis Potosí.

MP

I think the two scales bleed into each other. From the uppermost floor you have a 360-degree view of the city. And wherever you are in the city you can see the tower. As a result we had the intuition to groove the façade in order to blur the outline and emphasize the verticality.

MA

Also, from the adjacent streets, which are quite steep, an effect is produced like that when traveling past the Torres de Satélite in Mexico City. But looking at the project in more detail, we note that there is a double façade, which recalls industrial structures.

MC

First, we wanted to avoid at all cost the 'mirror-building' with the polarized glass curtain wall, like so many other office buildings in the area. Before specifying the materials, we were clear about the need for a scaffold-like surface that functioned like a screen.

SM

We thought that a glass façade is the simplest solution, but we were interested in the image of a scaffolding covering it, as if it were under repair. It's not so much a superimposed surface as a very slender steel building wrapped around the main structure.

MP

For this reason we wanted this scaffolding to function as a structure itself. We were interested in the scaffolding as a symbol of the mining activities in this area.

SM

We didn't want the scaffolding to be hanging from the building, but to be self-supporting, creating a space between interior and exterior.

MC

It is a kind of portico...

SM

One that recalls certain factory or industrial spaces...

MA

We might note a reference to the central BBVA building in Madrid, by Ábalos and Herreros, and their ideas on thermodynamics with its curved corners, though with greater thickness and less technological sophistication.

MC

It was also important that the spaces had a certain domestic condition, to allow users to go outside onto the terraces. Today, with COVID, we know that the model of hermetic glass boxes used by so many office buildings is no longer functional...

MA

Let's look at the main entrance to the building, the lobby that is also a plaza. Even once we're inside, the building remains public. In addition, the lobby ends with a solid, stone-built staircase that could have been there for centuries.

MC

From the outset, we didn't want it to be a building shut off from the city. The challenge was to create a permeable, open floor plan. The guiding spirit was to maintain continual contact with the exterior. We always had in mind the São Paulo buildings by Lina Bo Bardi and Paulo Mendes da Rocha, which don't seem to touch the ground.

MP

We also thought of the extraordinary Copan Building by Oscar Niemeyer in São Paulo, where the ground floor has an urban topography all its own, on a continuous gradient. The boundary between interior and exterior is not at all clear. Likewise, the large columns used in these reference points lie at the origins of our project.

MA

We could also point to the Cube Towers by Carme Pinós in Guadalajara, in terms of the way it reaches the ground and frees up the open, ambiguous space of the parking lot, or its lobby, which is a continuation of the public space that penetrates the building...

SM

Without question, the two Cube Towers are present in this project. We were involved in that project over a period of five years, when we worked as the local office for Carme Pinós. This reference point is a conscious one when it comes to the curves of the planters around the perimeter of the ground floor.

MC

Also present are the ones in the Igualada Cemetery by Enric Miralles and Pinós.

SM

And we can't deny the influence of Niemeyer. The other components that accompanied the building such as ramps, planters or staircases weren't working well with their straight lines and rectangles or boxes: the building's curved geometry complicated things. We realized that adding curves to the planters and staircases was the natural solution to this self-imposed condition.

MA

Did you adjust the perimeter outline as the excavation emerged?

MC

More than adjusting, we drew the outline right here, on site. We gradually determined the outline over the course of the eighteen months the excavation took.

MA

The floor plan was defined by the site, with the three bays around the central core. On the outside we have the façade that, like metal scaffolding, clings to the

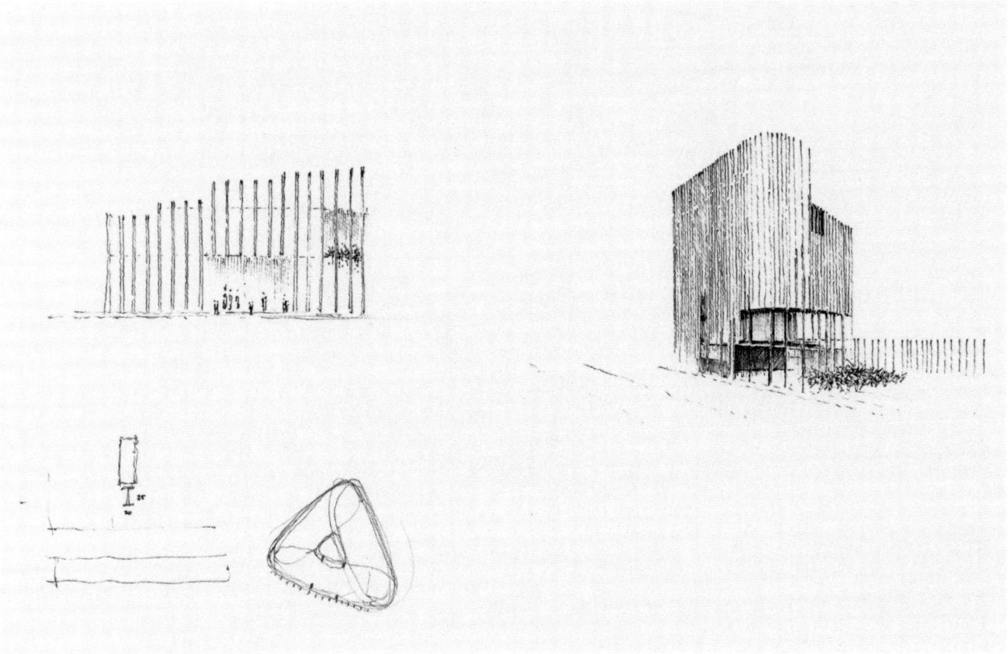

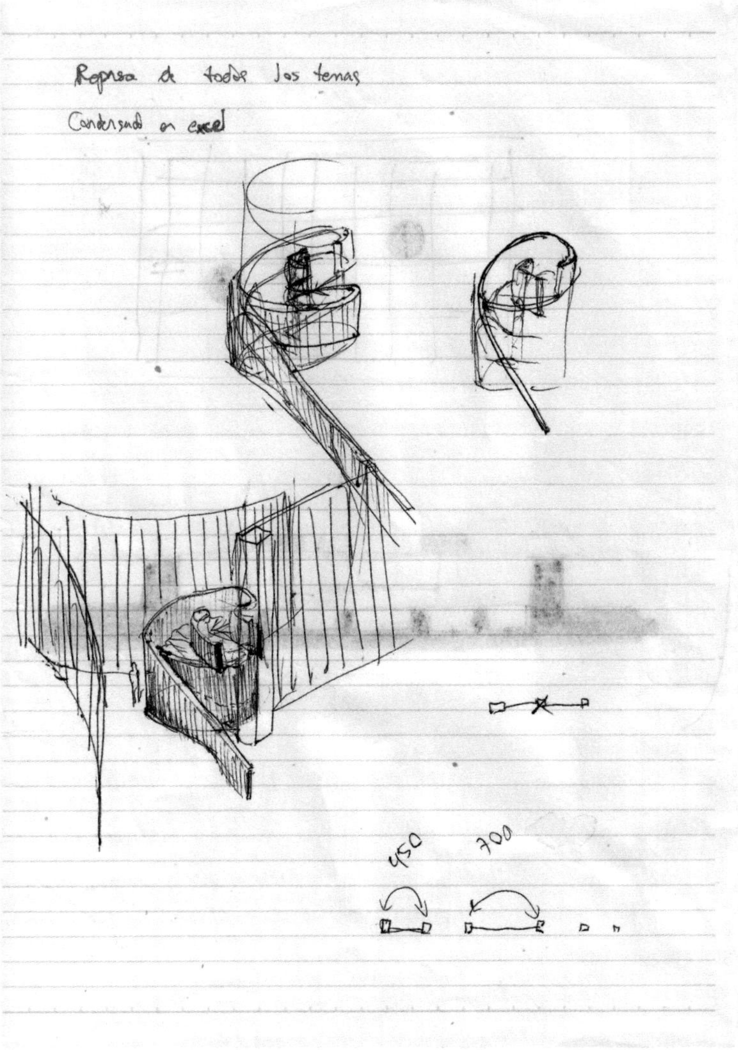
Repensa de todos los temas
Condensado en excel
450
700

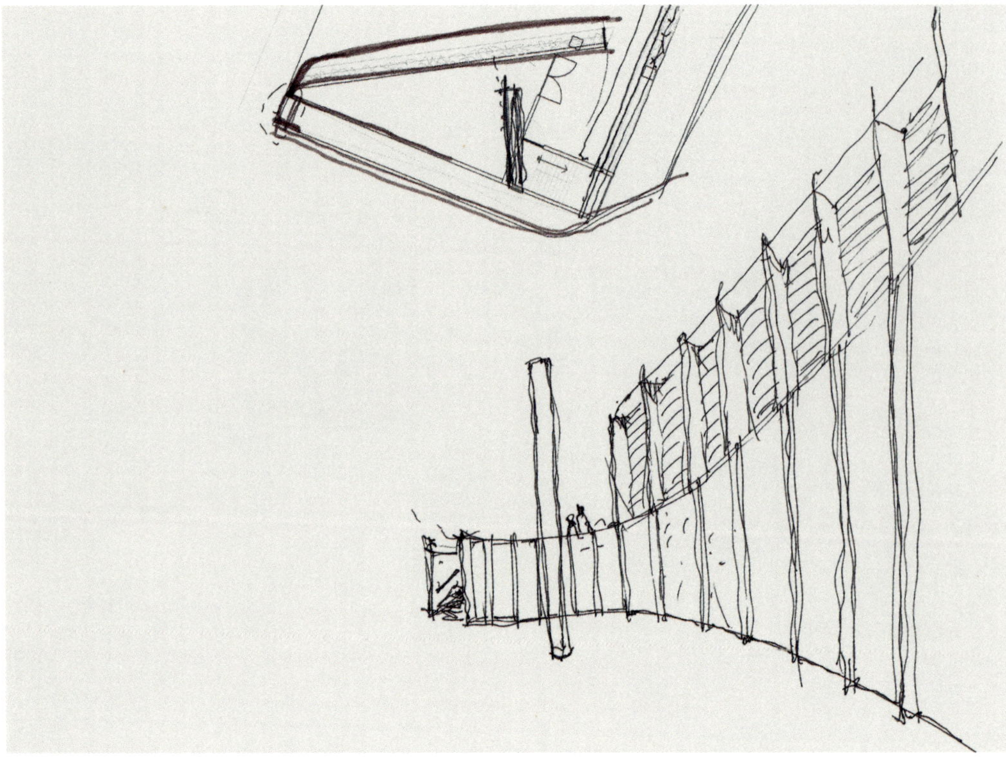

perimeter. Why then did you decide that the structure of the building should be concrete?

SM

Because of the curved geometry. From the outset, we wanted it to be a concrete structure because it is so much more malleable than steel. Thinking back to the curved cores of Carme Pinós' buildings, we decided that ours should also be concrete.

MP

There are even three different types of columns: rectangular, triangular and cylindrical. We paid attention to the structural demands, but also the geometric conditions the project asked of us. The relationship between each structural element and its form responds to its position within the curved core, as well as with the glass and aluminum façades.

MA

So, we have a concrete structure for the core and a double bay on each side. One red and one gray. What else made it possible to adapt the concrete to the specific needs of each area?

MC

We were treating the concrete as if it were stone, thinking about the stereotomy and color of stone. The concrete is the stone we wanted.

SM

There are concrete elements that are columns, or slabs, or pure structure within the office areas. In this sense, the columns along the perimeter of the offices are square in section because they have to support the façades. In contrast the ones that are visible beside the core are circular in section. In the lobby, the column comprises elements that are almost sculptural that not only bear weight but occupy the space. The structure also has a certain ornamental character.

MA

Why did you decide to groove the external walls of the core, and how did you hit upon the final finishes? Did you prepare mock-ups?

SM

On the one hand, the grooves enable us to retain the idea of verticality, while on the other they help with the curved formwork. We did a lot of samples. The grooves proved to be the natural way to make the curve. Metal shuttering and phenolic panels were prepared.

MP

It was a very striking sight when only the concrete structure was built, as you could see the huge gap between the perimeter of the site and the horizontal slabs. The height of the lobby is what enables you to appreciate the monumental proportions and embodies the relationship with the surroundings. In this way, the concrete skeleton clarified the architectural solution.

SM

I like to think the building was constructed out of architectural references. I'm very clear that the ramp in the basement references Mendes da Rocha, due to the way he liked to free up the columns from the slabs. References of this kind, images and drawings that we found and put on the table, were the way we shared what we were imagining. We had to persuade each other in order to advance. As for the basement, we recalled something that Alberto Kalach once remarked to us, when he observed that it was a shame that after all the effort that goes into excavating the ground for the basement stories, it is never a space that anyone wants to inhabit. In our case, we didn't want the basement to conceal the expression of the effort of that excavation—just like in a mine.

MA

It literally recalls San Luis Potosí's mining origins. Javier, how do you imagine occupying the space at the opposite end, on the top floor, where you'll have the best view of the city?

JG

It's a fact that we spend more time in the office than anywhere else, and we had to see how to improve the experience of the everyday. On the one hand there are the views, while on the other there are the terraces with their kiosks, natural light, eating areas in open spaces, all very pleasant. While we're talking about the work of these two excellent firms of architects, we should also mention that the result is thanks to the great efforts of so many others, such as the engineer who helped us to ground their crazy ideas in terms of dimensions and costs, the person responsible for the façade, the financial controller who found the

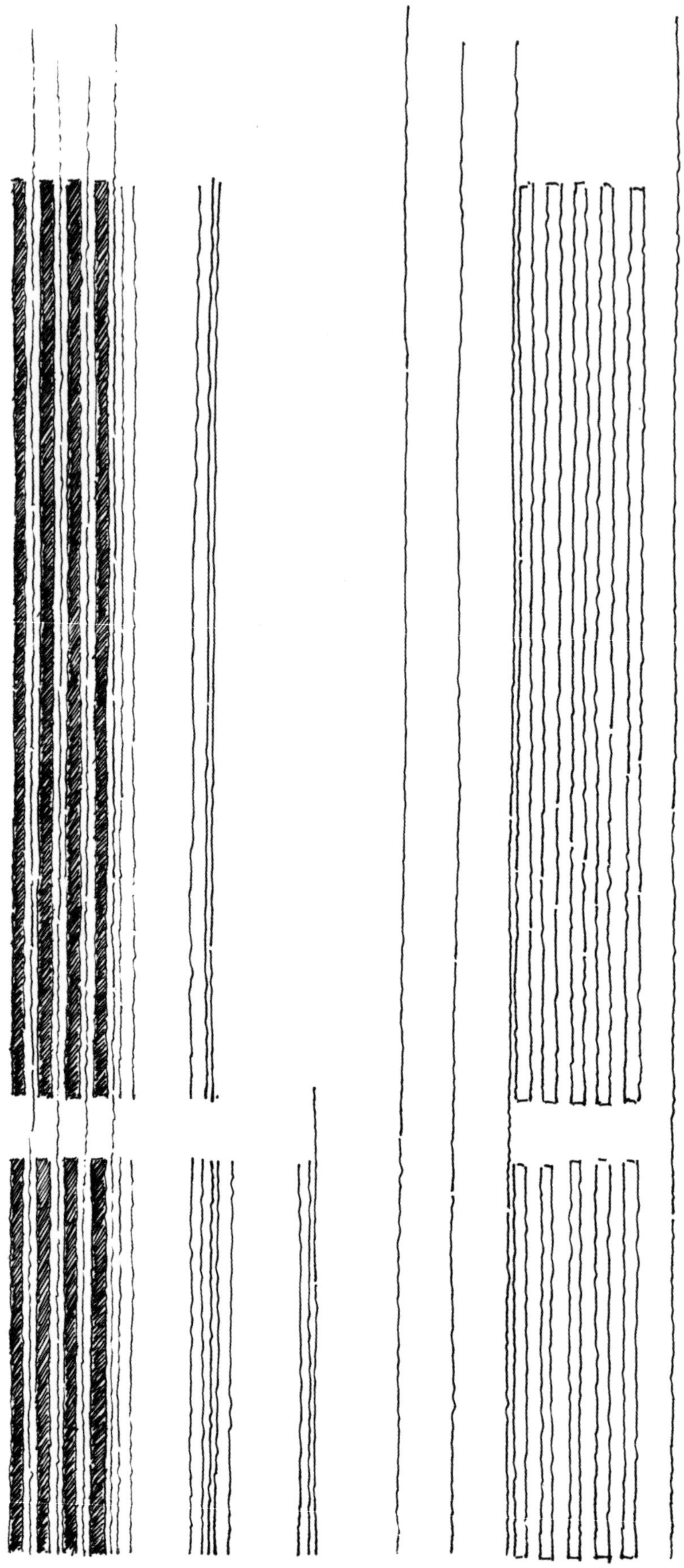

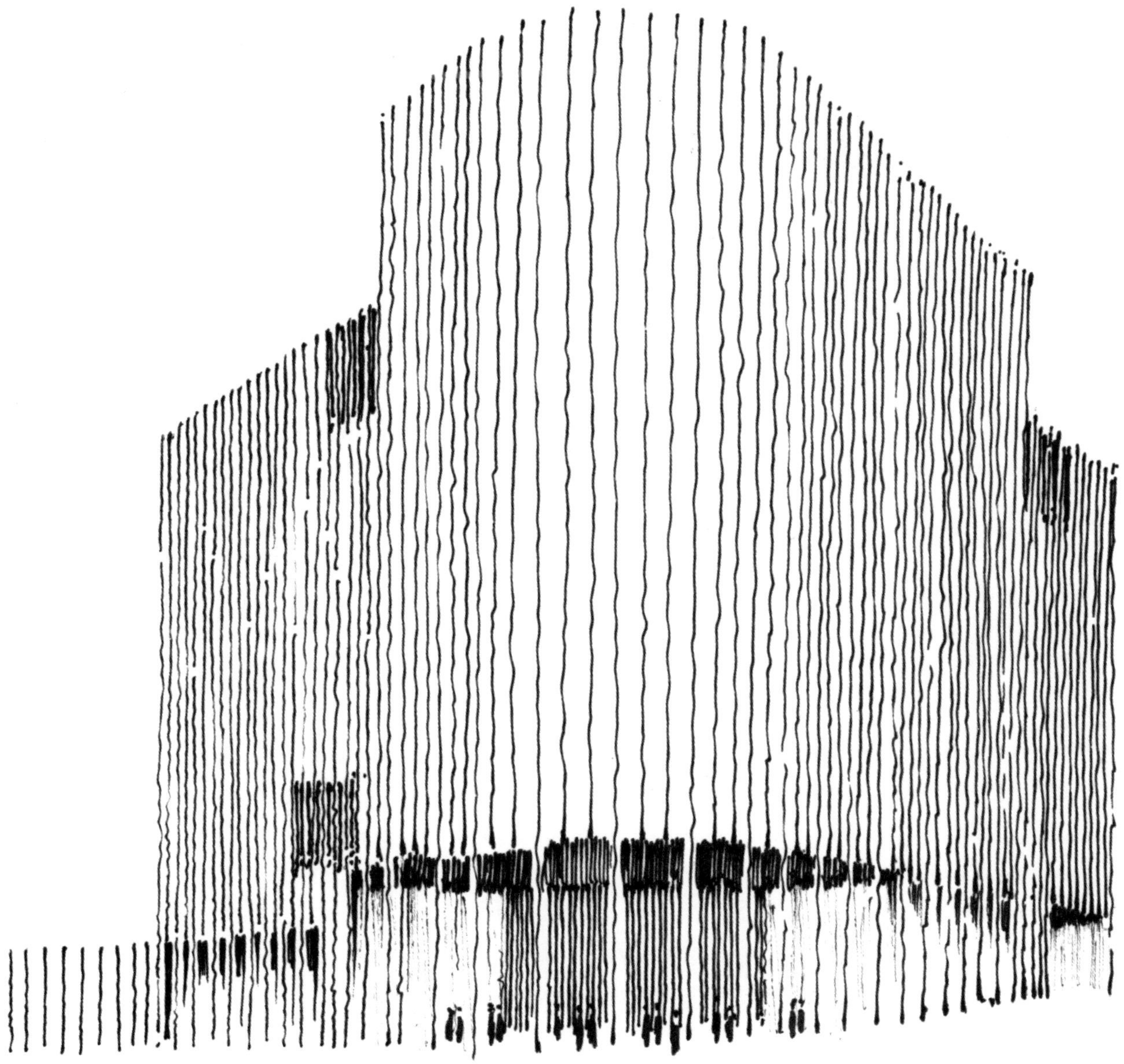

resources, all the efforts of the financier. Avancer Tower is the sum of all their efforts. The most visible aspect is the architecture, but it is only made possible by everything that was going on backstage.

SM

I think that if there is one thing this building contributes, it is the way it values the spaces we call basements. Almost all of us make use of them. The dignity we gave them was something we learned from Carme Pinós in Guadalajara. Basement floors should be important and potentially habitable spaces.

MP

Another aspect that should be highlighted is that the project is the result of multiple efforts by many people who were focused on doing things well. Just imagine how much could be done in this country by uniting our efforts, as we did in this project, with the alliance of families and clients.

MC

The greatest value for us are the relationships we formed along the way. The relationship among ourselves, with Javier and his family, and with Magui and Salvador. Hegel said that if something lacked spirit it would not endure. If that had not happened here, it wouldn't have come out this way.

JG

Don't forget that even before the building was finished, it already brought together couples who will marry (the family of the crane operator), as well as the girl who comes here to sing and dance cumbia...

MC

It would be interesting to present recent experiences that show how even before the building was inaugurated it had already become a part of San Luis Potosí. The people made it their own.

SM

I feel that for all of us it's been like what happened with Mathias Goeritz, Josef Albers or yourself, Miquel, when you came to Mexico, all people who arriving from outside swiftly see what is unique about a place and know right away what to highlight and what needs work. We were the foreigners here. We worked with the local materials. We like to think that architecture is a cultural object. We love seeing how the local people quickly identified with the Avancer building, and are glad to think that the building doesn't belong to us as architects, nor even to the owner or the occupants: it belongs to this city. Our goal is for the local people to make it theirs.

EDIFICIO SAN LUIS POTOSI, LA TECTONICA DEL ANDAMIAJE COMO ELEMENTO CONSTRUCTIVO DE LA FACHADA.

The layout of the project is determined by a structural grid that helps to rationalize the irregular geometry of the site, and efficiently resolve the arrangement and circulation of the cars in the basement parking lots. The first floor of the building is conceived as an open-plan space permitting pedestrian flows that bring the building closer to the street. On this level, the commercial program is broken down into blocks independent from the structural system of the tower, maintaining its permeable character.

The office floors are configured by two slightly offset bays with a vertical circulation nucleus at the center. The resulting outline of the building is slender on its east and west sides and elongated on its north and south façades. On the latter, the repetition of vertical concrete elements helps to control solar gain.

Pigmented concrete columns and slabs make up the structural system. The pigment used for the concrete mimics the natural stone hue of the site, which is an important aspect of the city's colonial architectural identity.

On each office floor, terraces and small gardens provide users with sites of interaction and gathering. The south bay is interrupted to form a terrace on the eighth floor, and on the top floor of the north bay the concrete structure is extended to create a green roof with endemic vegetation.

Plans

Context

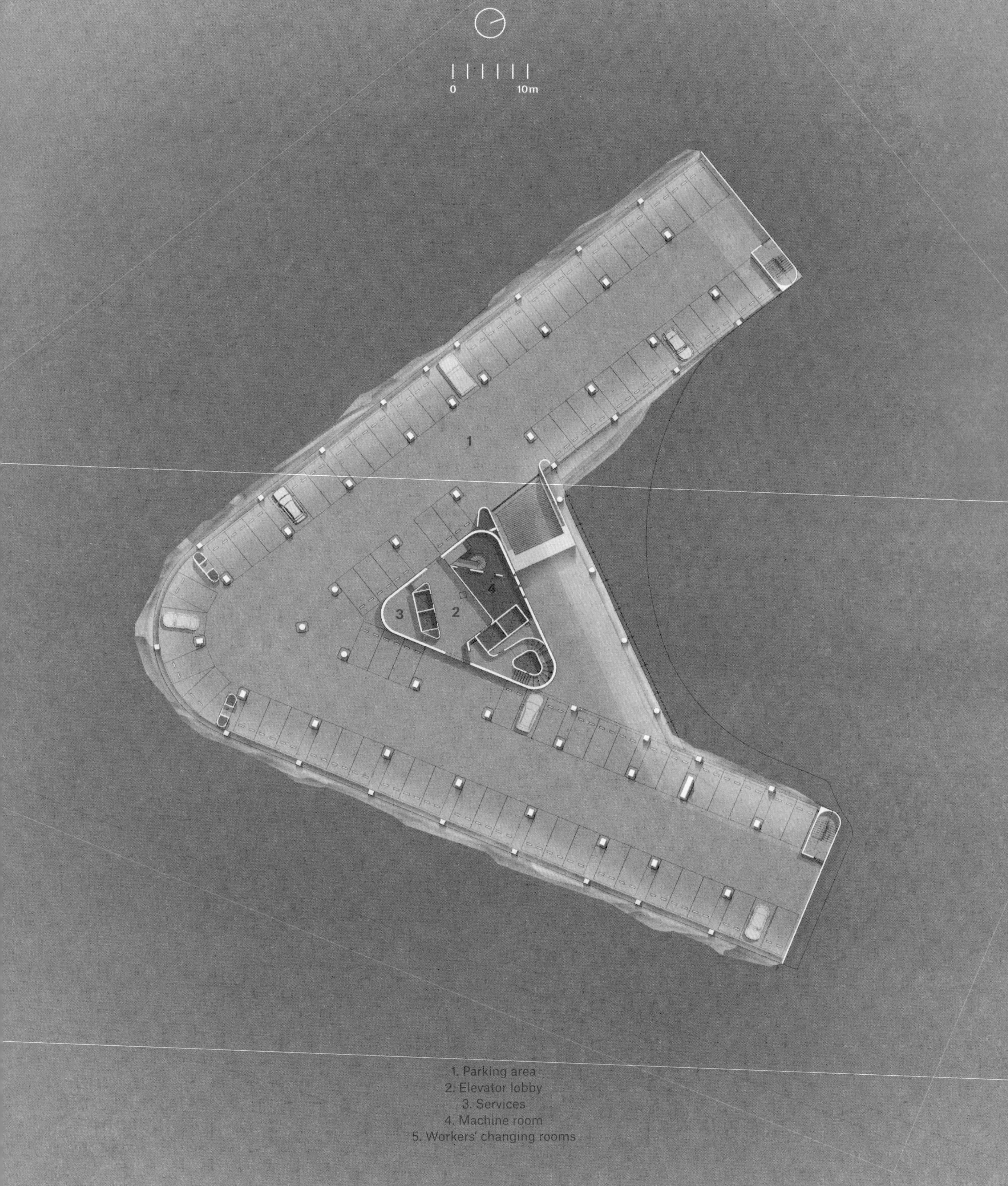

1. Parking area
2. Elevator lobby
3. Services
4. Machine room
5. Workers' changing rooms

Basement 4

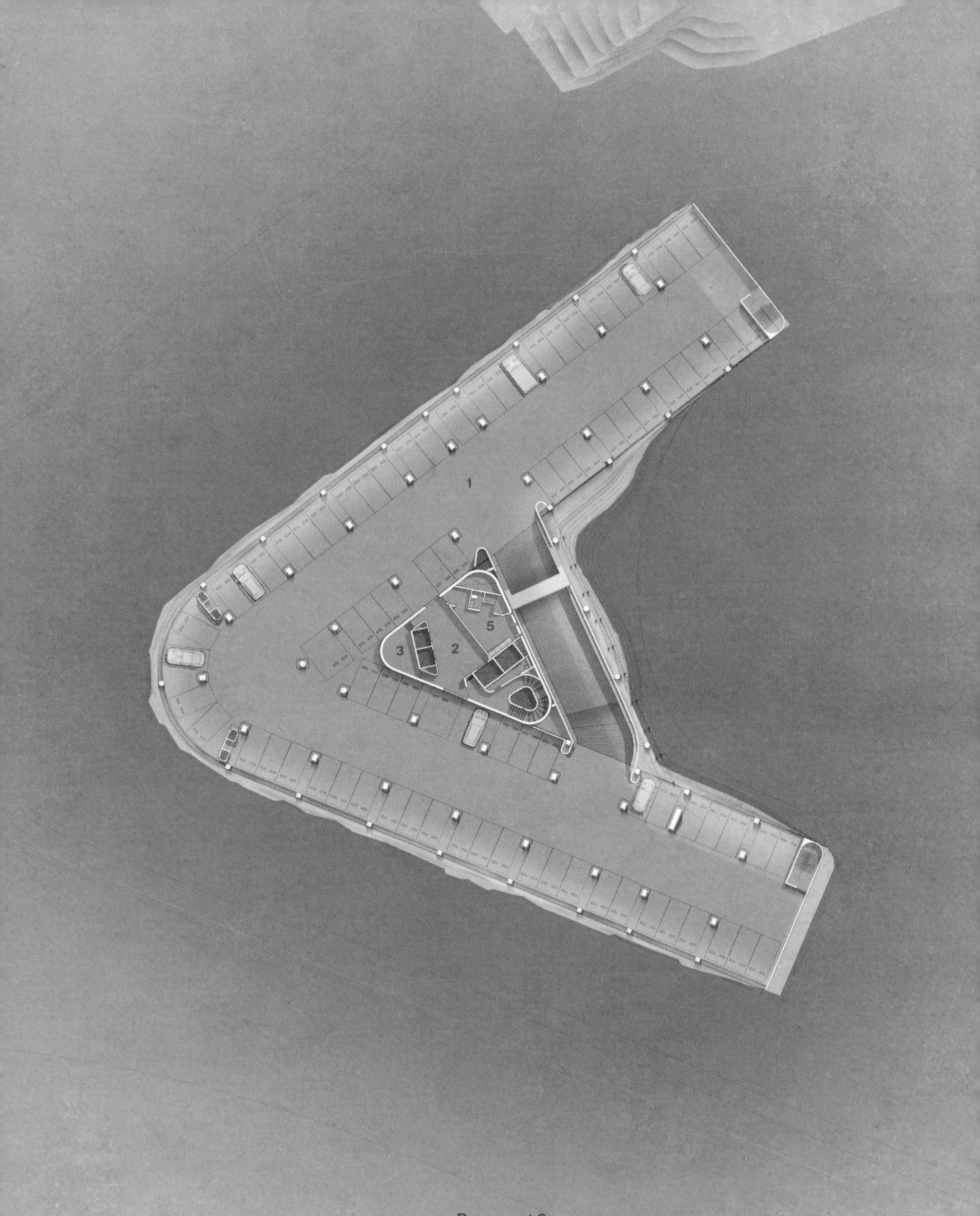

Basement 3

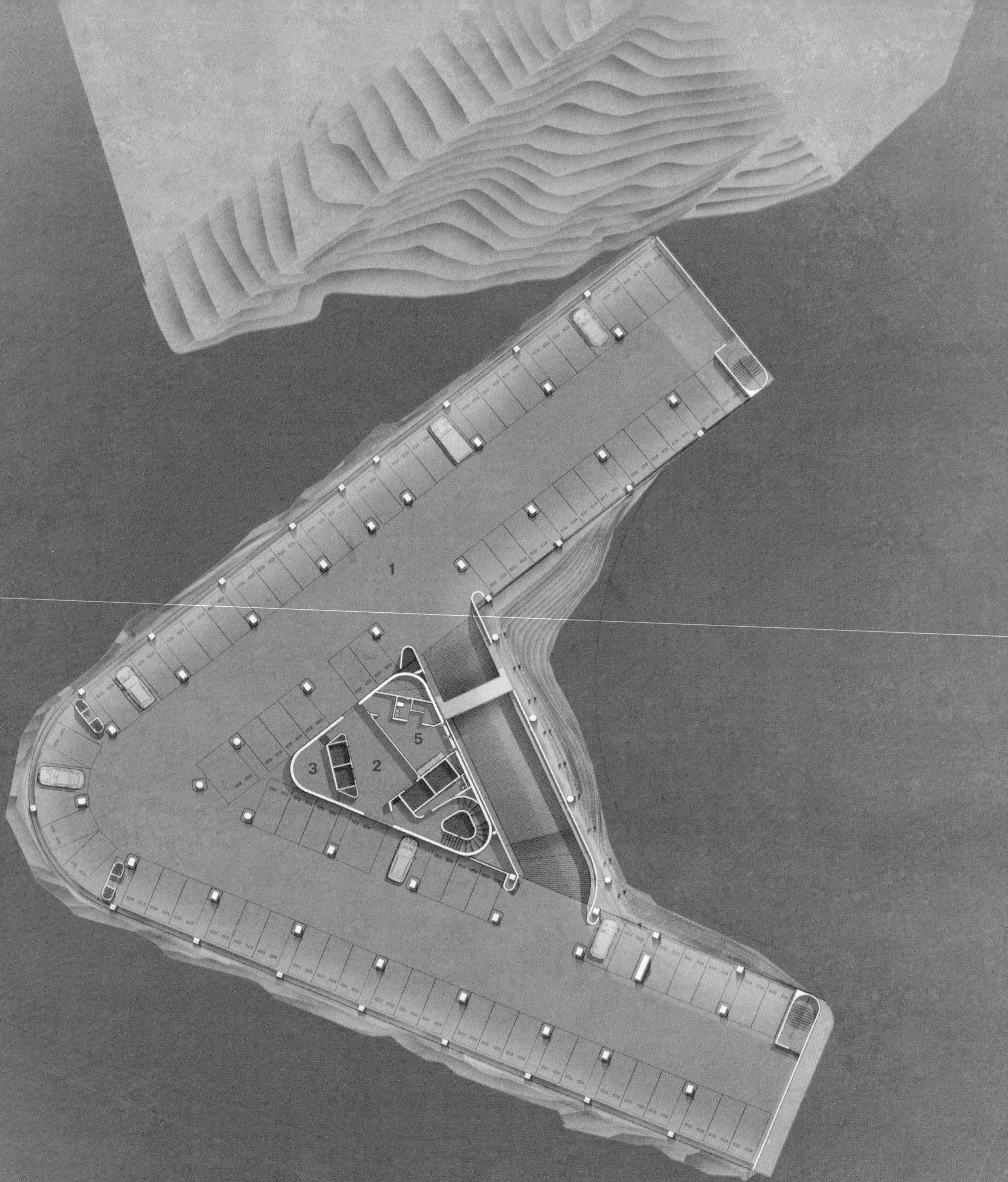

1. Parking area
2. Elevator lobby
3. Services
5. Workers' changing rooms
6. Site
7. Bathrooms
8. Vehicle entrance
12. Store
13. Terrace

Basement 2

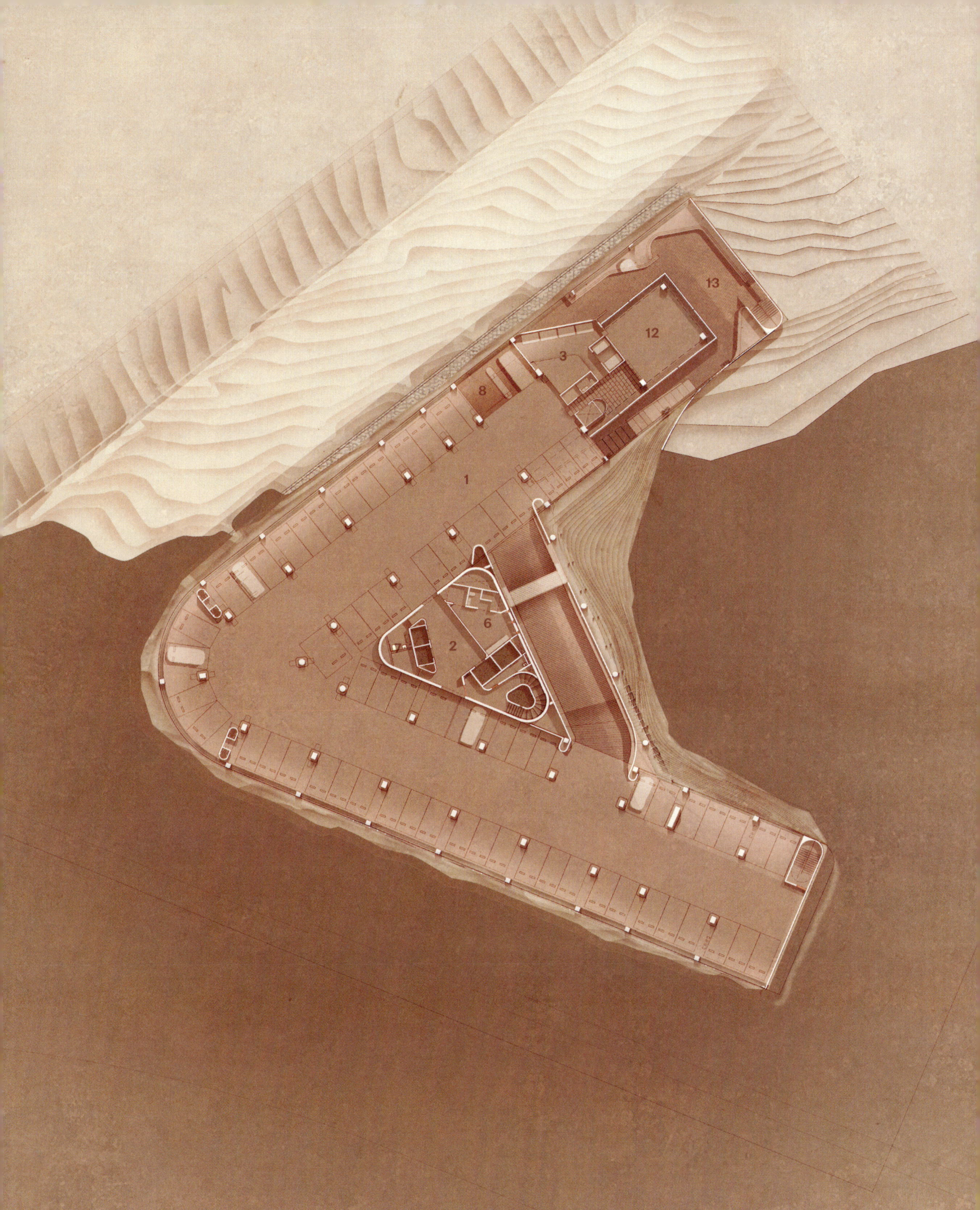

Basement 1

1. Parking area
2. Elevator lobby
3. Services
7. Bathrooms
8. Vehicle entrance
9. Main entrance
10. Secondary entrance
11. Main lobby
12. Store
13. Terrace
14. Electrical control room

Ground floor plan

Mezzanine

2. Elevator lobby
7. Bathrooms
13. Terrace
15. Offices

Level 1

Level 2

2. Elevator lobby
7. Bathrooms
13. Terrace
15. Offices

Level 3

Level 4

2. Elevator lobby
7. Bathrooms
13. Terrace
15. Offices

Level 5

Level 6

2. Elevator lobby
7. Bathrooms
13. Terrace
15. Offices

Level 7

Level 10

3. Services
15. Offices
16. Rooftop

Level 11

Rooftop plan

Section

Section

Excavation

Structure

Enclosures

A 100 m
40

Macías Peredo

Macías Peredo is an architecture firm founded by Salvador Macías Corona (Guadalajara, 1977) and Magui Peredo Arenas (Guadalajara, 1979), graduates of the Instituto Tecnológico y de Estudios Superiores de Occidente (ITESO) in the city of Guadalajara, Mexico, where they have been project workshop professors for several years.

As Macías Peredo they have presented numerous lectures on their professional practice in different universities and forums in Mexico and abroad, including at the University of Columbia in New York, the University of New Mexico in Albuquerque, the University of Texas in Arlington, the University of Washington in Seattle, Rice University in Houston and the GSD at Harvard University, Massachusetts; the University of Tokyo in Japan; the Catholic University in Chile, the Peruvian University of Applied Sciences (UPC) in Lima; at the Bogotá International Art Fair 2018 (ARTBO), the AbrA Architecture Encounters in Medellín, Colombia, the Quito Pan-American Architecture Biennale, Ecuador, the Brasilia College of Architects, Brazil, as well as the College of Architects of Mendoza, Argentina, and in the framework of MantovArchitettura 2019 in Mantua, Italy.

They won second place in the competition for the Mexico Pavilion at Expo Shanghai 2010, and first place in the El Eco Pavilion 2013 in Mexico City. In 2014 they were awarded the Emerging Voices prize by The Architectural League of New York. They exhibited their work at LIGA, Espacio de Arquitectura in Mexico City in 2015. They were finalists for the 'Mies Crown Hall Americas Prize' exhibition organized by the Illinois Institute of Technology (IIT) and the College of Architecture, in Chicago. They participated in the Mexico Pavilion at the Venice Biennale of Architecture 2018, and in the show 'Diseñando México. Architettura: Necessità e Libertà' at MantovArchitettura 2019. They were finalists for the Works Panorama of the 11th Ibero-American Biennale of Architecture and Urbanism, and selected to participate in the Mexico Pavilion at the Venice Biennale of Architecture 2020.

Their first monograph, *To Still the Noise*, was published in 2017 by Arquine, and in 2020 AMAG published a second book showcasing their most recent work.

MOMA San Francisco acquired the model, sketches and materials from the project Casa Escondida in Puerto Escondido in Oaxaca for his private collection.

In addition to their professional practice they run the architecture exhibition space Jardín 17 in the Luis Barragán Home and Studio in Mexico City. Recently, Diego Quirarte has joined the studio as a partner.

Manuel Cervantes Estudio

Manuel Cervantes Céspedes (Mexico City, 1977) graduated as an architect from Anáhuac University, and is a member of the National Academy of Architecture and of the National Art Creators System (FONCA). He established Manuel Cervantes Estudio in 2004.

The studio has developed projects on a range of scales in America, Europe and the Middle East with housing, hotel, transport, mixed use, commercial, sports and cultural typologies. It has partnered with a number of authorities on small and large-scale projects ranging from rural housing to multimodal transport centers.

He has received numerous awards, including first prize in the public contest for the Azteca Multimodal Terminal project in the State of Mexico (2006), first prize in the public contest for the El Rosario Transport Interchange project (2009), first prize in the 10th Biennial of Architecture ICCYC (Costa Rican Institute of Cement and Concrete) for El Mirador Pavilion and for El Rosario Transport Interchange and the Equestrian project (2010), silver medal in the 11th Biennial of Mexican Architecture (2010), silver medal at the First Architecture Biennial of Mexico City (2013), the Luis Barragán Award for Professional Career 2013, awarded by the CAM-SAM (College and Society of Architects of the Mexico City), the International Award of the 19th Pan-American Architecture Biennial of Quito (2014), silver medal at the 13th Mexican Architecture Biennial for the Equestrian Project (2014), the Emerging Voices Award granted by the Architectural League of New York (2015), the silver medal at the 14th Mexican Architecture Biennial for Housing in Amatepec and for the Next Hydroponic Plant (2015), the silver medal at the third Biennial of Architecture of Mexico City for Housing in Amatepec and for the Cuatro Caminos Transport Interchange (2017), the silver medal at the 14th National Architecture Biennial for Casa Avándaro and Ecuestre Puebla (2018) and the Silver medal at the 15th National Architecture Biennial for Rural Housing Salazar (2020), and he was a finalist in the 3rd Oscar Niemeyer Award for Casa Avándaro (2020).

His work has been published in three monographs: *Manuel Cervantes. CC Arquitectos* (Arquine, 2015); *El Croquis* (2018); and *Manuel Cervantes Estudio* (TC Cuadernos, 2021), and has been shown at the exhibitions 'Rural Tectonics' at the Design Gallery in Miami (2018) and 'Praxis' at the Museo de San Ildefonso in Mexico City (2019).

Manuel Cervantes Céspedes, Salvador Macías Corona and Magui Peredo Arenas

Credits

Architects
Manuel Cervantes Céspedes
Salvador Macías Corona
Magui Peredo Arenas

Design team
Nuno Pinto
Diego Flores
Ángel García
Ana Padrón
Jacobo Mendoza
Diego Quirarte
Andrea Amaral

Constructed surface area
27,530 m^2

Plot area
3,395 m^2

Location
San Luis Potosí, México

Year
2017–2021

Structural engineering
Ceromotion - Ingeniería Estructural y Protección Sísmica

Electrical and hydraulic engineering
diin - Ingeniería

Façade engineering
Grupo Básica

Construction
Structure: Stärken Group
Façades: Grupo Básica
Carpentry: dk mobel
Ironwork: Arial 10 Arquitectos
Flooring: cosip / Artec
HVAC: Cíclope
Fire protection: Grupo Philadelphia
Special installations: Speqtrum
Elevators: Mitsubishi

Coordination
Alfredo Reyes
Juan Carlos Malagón

Avancer was printed and bound in August 2022 by Asia Pacific Offset in Hong Kong, China. It was printed on 80 gsm Enso Classic paper and set in typefaces of the Garamond Premier Pro and Atlas families, designed by Robert Slimbach and Susana Carvalho, Kai Bernau and Christian Schwartz, respectively. The print run was 700 copies. ////